# NATIONAL AUDUBON SOCIETY
## POCKET GUIDES

**National Audubon Society**

*The mission of the* NATIONAL AUDUBON SOCIETY *is to conserve and restore natural ecosystems, focusing on birds and other wildlife for the benefit of humanity and the Earth's biological diversity.*

We have nearly 600,000 members and an extensive chapter network, plus a staff of scientists, lobbyists, lawyers, policy analysts, and educators. Through our sanctuaries we manage 150,000 acres of critical habitat.

Our award-winning *Audubon* magazine carries outstanding articles and color photography on wildlife, nature, and the environment. We also publish *American Birds,* an ornithological journal, *Audubon Activist,* a newsjournal, and *Audubon Adventures,* a newsletter reaching 500,000 elementary school students. Our *World of Audubon* television shows air on TBS and public television.

For information about how you can become a member, please write or call the Membership Department at:

NATIONAL AUDUBON SOCIETY
700 Broadway, New York, New York 10003
(212) 979-3000

# SONGBIRDS AND FAMILIAR BACKYARD BIRDS
## (*Western Region*)

**Text by Richard K. Walton**

**Alfred A. Knopf, New York**

This is a Borzoi Book
Published by Alfred A. Knopf, Inc.

Copyright © 1994 Chanticleer Press, Inc.
All rights reserved.
Published in the United States by Alfred A. Knopf, Inc.,
New York, and simultaneously in Canada by Random House
of Canada Limited, Toronto.  Distributed by Random
House, Inc., New York.

Prepared and produced by Chanticleer Press, Inc.,
New York.
Printed and bound by Dai Nippon Printing Co., Ltd., Tokyo.

Published February 1994
First Printing

Library of Congress Catalog Number: 93-21254
ISBN: 0-679-74925-X

# Contents

## How to Use This Guide

One of the many pleasures of birdwatching involves not watching, but listening, to the cheerful trill of a warbler, the sad coo of the Mourning Dove, or the clear warble of the House Finch. Even in urban areas, a surprising variety of songbirds—and other fascinating species—may be encountered by a watchful observer. This guide is designed to help you identify many familiar western birds and learn more about their habits.

Coverage

This book features 80 species of songbirds and other birds frequently observed in urban and suburban areas of western North America. The region covered extends roughly from the Pacific Ocean east to the Great Plains. A companion volume in the National Audubon Society Pocket Guide series covers species east of these boundaries. The birds are presented in the American Ornithologists' Union's taxonomic order.

Organization

There are three parts to this guide: introductory essays; color plates and accompanying descriptions; and appendices.

Introduction

The essay called "Birdwatching" discusses some of the reasons why the pastime is so popular and offers tips on equipment that can enhance the experience. "Identifying

6

Birds" outlines what to notice when you look at a bird, and "Western Birds" describes the bird families represented in this guide. Finally, there are suggestions for attracting birds to your yard and a message about bird conservation.

The Birds  This section contains photographs of 80 species of birds in their natural habitats. Facing each photograph is a description of the species, beginning with a discussion of its unique or unusual traits. The paragraph labeled "Identification" gives a bird's adult size and field marks; its voice, habitat, and range are described in the sections that follow. To supplement each range statement, there is a map on which breeding and winter ranges are indicated by diagonal hatching. Where there is an overlap, or wherever a species occurs year-round, the ranges are superimposed.

Breeding range

Winter range

Permanent range

Accompanying each account is a small silhouette, designed as an aid in identification. These silhouettes represent general body types but do not necessarily indicate the subtle variations that can occur among species of the same family.

Appendices  Following the photographs is a drawing of a familiar bird, labelled with the terms used to describe field marks. The glossary defines additional terms that may be unfamiliar.

## Birdwatching

Birdwatching is a fast-growing and enormously popular pastime. Estimates suggest that between 60 and 80 million people are involved with "birding" to some extent. Many of these enthusiasts are backyard birdwatchers; others regularly travel far afield to regional parks, conservation areas, and birding "hot spots." Many birders join in organized bird walks, censusing projects, and fund-raising activities for their local conservation organizations. Typical of this group are the more than 42,000 birders who participate in over 2,000 National Audubon Society–Leica Christmas Bird Counts and National Audubon Society Birdathons, held annually throughout North America. Even more people enjoy birds as a complement to other activities, such as gardening, hiking, jogging, boating, and fishing.

Why do so many people watch birds? There may be as many answers to this question as there are birders. In general, however, birds are diverse, colorful, readily observable, and reasonably easy to identify. Another important attraction may be the relative simplicity of birding. Once you are equipped with a bird guide and binoculars, you are ready to begin. Yet this simple beginning may contain the seeds of a lifelong passion.

Binoculars   A decent pair of binoculars can enhance your enjoyment of birds considerably. If you already own binoculars, "field test" them to see if they are suitable for birdwatching. Check for clarity of image and ease of focus. If you don't own good binoculars, consider investing some time and money to learn about and buy a reliable pair.

There are books on how to buy binoculars, and you may wish to consult one, but a few basic facts will get you started. Specifications for binoculars are stated in a form that includes two numerals separated by a multiplication sign: for example, $7 \times 35$. The first numeral refers to overall magnification; the second, to the diameter (in millimeters) of the objective lens (the lens closest to the object you are observing). So, in this example, the binocular magnifies the image seven times and has an objective lens that is 35 millimeters wide. If you divide the second numeral by the first, the result is what is called the "exit pupil." The exit pupil in this example is 5. It gives you a relative idea of how much light reaches the eye. A $10 \times 40$ binocular has an exit pupil of 4, indicating that less light will reach the eye.

Beyond these specifications, comparisons tend to become more difficult. An inexpensive pair of binoculars might have

9

a high exit pupil but poor optics. On the other hand, some excellent binoculars have a relatively low exit pupil but provide a clear, bright image because of their exceptional optics and lens coating. Fine binoculars combine high-quality optics with durable construction. At publication, top-grade binoculars cost anywhere from $600 to $1,000. However, very acceptable mid-range binoculars, such as several Bausch and Lomb models endorsed by the National Audubon Society, may be bought for $200 to $500.

Spotting Scopes    Certain groups of birds, such as raptors and shorebirds, are better observed with spotting scopes, which are similar to telescopes mounted on tripods. These scopes provide higher magnification than most binoculars; the tripods provide the stability necessary with increased magnification. Depending on the quality of their optics and housings, prices range between $200 and $1,000. The tripod should be chosen for its stability and portability. Avoid spending so much on a scope that you have to settle for a "make-do" tripod. An acceptable scope and tripod will cost about $300.

**Identifying Birds**

Many beginning birdwatchers have had the experience of spending time with a seasoned birder who correctly identifies every flitting feather with miraculous ease. Despite outward appearances, the expert has no superhuman abilities. His or her expertise has developed over time. Given the same time and practice, you can develop similar skills.

Range An important first step in correctly identifying birds is knowing what birds to expect, as well as when and where to expect them. A state bird list, available from your local chapter of the National Audubon Society, will be useful. This Pocket Guide will also help you narrow down the possibilities. Browse through the guide, noting the ranges of the various species, including their seasonal distributions.

Size A notion of the overall size of a bird is a critical component of identification. Each species account in this guide includes the body length (from tip of bill to tip of tail) of the bird. Perhaps just as useful are comparative descriptions such as "sparrow-sized" or "crow-sized." Field experience with benchmark species such as the Song Sparrow, American Robin, Blue Jay, American Crow, and Canada Goose will prepare you to use their general sizes in a comparative way.

Shape     Some birds can be identified by their shapes alone. In the field, under various light conditions, a silhouette may be all that is discernible. As you gain experience, you will be able to use overall proportions as well as the specific shapes of bills, heads, and tails to confirm a bird's identity.

Color and Pattern     The colorful feathers of many birds are important identifying characteristics. More often than not, however, it is a combination of color and pattern that confirms a bird's identity. Experts use a somewhat specialized vocabulary to describe these field marks. Terms such as crown, eye-stripe, eye-ring, and undertail are readily understandable. Other terms such as mandible, speculum, and undertail coverts require explanation. To become familiar with such terms, refer to the illustration and glossary at the back of this guide.

Behavior     Behavioral clues are also useful for identification. Some birds habitually flick their tails, others scratch among the leaves, and still others bob their heads up and down. Typical behavior is mentioned in the general description or under "Identification" in each species account.

Voice     Beginners should spend some time learning the songs and calls of birds. Virtually all North American birds can be identified by voice alone. Each species account in this Pocket Guide includes a section on "Voice." Both descriptive terms and phonetic clues are given. These calls and songs are not only enjoyable to learn but they can also be very useful in places such as dense woodlands and extensive thickets. A variety of commercial products are available to help you learn bird songs.

Gestalt  Experienced observers use any or all of the clues mentioned above, often in combination with a process of elimination, to identify birds. At times a flick of the tail, a single call note, a flash of color, or a familiar silhouette is enough to confirm an identification. More often a combination of factors reveals the species. At times, birdwatchers refer to the "jizz," or gestalt, of a bird—some overall look or impression that may be difficult to analyze but somehow suggests the given species. Most likely, jizz or gestalt is simply a combination of the various factors outlined here. Ultimately, it is time in the field that will enable you to develop your identification skills.

## Western Birds

The 100th meridian, extending through the Great Plains, forms the traditional dividing line between eastern and western North America. The continental land mass west of this line is significantly larger than that to the east. Perhaps even more important for the birdwatcher is the fact that in the western region of the country the diversity of habitats is relatively greater than in the East. Included among important western habitats are a variety of freshwater wetlands, short-grass prairies, badlands, foothills, mountains, deserts, coniferous forests, chaparral, and coastal beaches and dunes, as well as their associated brackish wetlands. Each of these habitats, from the deserts of the Southwest to the arctic-alpine peaks of the Rocky Mountains, provides resources for a variety of bird species. The requirements of some species are strict and unvarying, but other birds are adapted to a broader range of conditions, including those that exist in many western backyards.

This volume presents 80 common species of western birds, many of which are regularly found in well-planted neighborhoods. The majority of species are from a large group of birds normally referred to as songbirds. Included among the songbirds covered here are many familiar jays, nuthatches, thrushes, warblers, sparrows, orioles, and finches. In addition, you will find representatives of other groups of birds that, while technically not songbirds, are also familiar denizens of backyards. These include a variety of doves, hummingbirds, and woodpeckers. A companion guide, the *National Audubon Society Pocket Guide to Songbirds and Familiar Backyard Birds (Eastern Region),* covers similarly selected species that occur in the eastern United States.

Bird Families

In this guide, 30 different bird families and subfamilies are represented, some by only a single species and others by two or more. Birds are grouped into families based upon structural characteristics, genetic similarity, vocalizations, and behavior. Knowing the characteristics of these groups is one way to simplify the process of identifying an unfamiliar species.

Hawks and Falcons

Hawks (family Accipitridae) and falcons (Falconidae) are predatory birds with strong, hooked beaks, strong talons, and keen eyesight. They typically feed on small mammals, other birds, or large insects. Accipiters rely on stealth and surprise in order to capture small birds. Falcons prefer open-country hunting, in which they use their slim, pointed wings to outfly their prey or to hover in the open before dropping on an unsuspecting victim.

Quail, Pigeons, and Doves — Quail (Phasianidae) are plump, chickenlike birds that spend most of their time walking on the ground, scratching for seeds and insects. Many quail have loud and distinctive calls, and nearly all species are popular as game birds. Pigeons and doves (Columbidae) are round-bodied, small-headed, and fast-flying. Their cooing calls are occasionally mistaken for those of owls, and they usually feed by walking slowly on the ground.

Cuckoos — Cuckoos (Cuculidae) are slim, long-tailed, and reclusive. The Roadrunner, our largest cuckoo, spends much of its time on the ground.

Hummingbirds — The tiny, long-billed, energetic hummingbirds (Trochilidae) have iridescent plumage. They are able to hover in flight and are most often observed feeding on the nectar of brightly colored flowers.

Woodpeckers — Woodpeckers (Picidae) are tree-climbers that use their stiffened tails as props while they dig out insects and grubs from decaying tree bark with their long, chisel-like bills.

| | |
|---|---|
| Flycatchers | Flycatchers (Tyrannidae) are big-headed, large-billed birds that capture flying insects by making periodic aerial sallies from a conspicuous perch. Many species are best identified by their distinctive call notes. |
| Swallows | The swallows (Hirundinidae) are serial feeders that spend most of their time on the wing, pursuing flying insects. Many species nest near human habitations. During migration, huge numbers may be seen together. |
| Jays, Crows, and Magpies | The familiar jays, crows, and magpies (Corvidae) are large, noisy, intelligent birds. Unlike many birds, they are practically omnivorous. |
| Verdins and Nuthatches | Verdins (Remizidae) are similar in appearance and behavior to the members of the chickadee and titmouse family (Paridae). Nuthatches (Sittidae) are small bark-gleaners, often seen clambering head-downward over the trunks and limbs of trees. They often associate with chickadees and titmice at birdfeeders. |
| Wrens | Wrens (Troglodytidae) are small, loud, brown birds that normally carry their stubby tails over their backs. Many wrens readily nest in birdhouses. |

| | |
|---|---|
| Kinglets | Kinglets, gnatcatchers (subfamily Sylviinae), thrushes (subfamily Turdinae), and Wrentits (subfamily Chamaeinae) all belong to the large family Muscicapidae. Diminutive and very active, kinglets are often found in association with chickadees or warblers. Gnatcatchers resemble slim, long-tailed warblers because of their energetic behavior and sharp, pointed bills. Thrushes, including the familiar robin, are fine songsters that prefer to dwell in shaded forests, where they feed on berries and insects. The Wrentit is the sole member of its subfamily. |
| Mimic Thrushes | Slim and long-tailed, mimic thrushes (Mimidae) typically have complex songs that often incorporate imitations of other birds' songs. They often forage on the ground. |
| Waxwings | The waxwings (Bombycillidae) are gregarious wanderers that move irregularly about in search of berries. Colorful waxy tips on their secondaries give them their name. |
| Silky Flycatchers | Silky flycatchers (Ptilogonatidae) are represented in North America by a single species, the Phainopepla. The adjective "silky" refers to their smooth feathers. |
| Starlings and Vireos | The starlings (Sturnidae), from a Old World family, are an introduced species and now one of our most common birds. |

Starlings are fine mimics of other birds' songs. Vireos (Vireonidae) are small woodland birds that resemble sluggish, thick-billed warblers. They often may be located in the forest canopy by their persistent songs.

Emberizids Emberizids (Emberizidae) are such a diverse group that they have no common name. Some of the more important emberizid subfamilies include the wood-warblers (Parulinae); tanagers (Thraupinae); cardinals, grosbeaks, and buntings (Cardinalinae); towhees and sparrows (Emberizinae); and blackbirds (Icterinae).

Wood-warblers Small, brightly colored, and animated, the insect-eating wood-warblers have variable songs, spectacular migrations, and interesting behavior that make them among the most popular birds in the New World.

Tanagers Tanagers are sluggish canopy-dwellers whose bright colors and rich songs are reminiscent of the tropical forests where most members of this subfamily occur.

Cardinals Cardinals, buntings, grosbeaks, and sparrows are subfamilies that generally include talented songsters with thick, conical bills used for eating seeds. Sparrows tend to be conservatively plumaged, while cardinals, buntings,

19

and grosbeaks include some of North America's most colorful species.

**Blackbirds and Orioles**  Blackbirds and orioles typically have sharp-pointed bills, and include many species that are beautiful songsters.

**Cardueline Finches**  Closely related to the emberizids, cardueline finches (Fringillidae) are brightly colored seed-eaters that readily visit backyard birdfeeders during the winter.

**Weavers**  An Old World species, weavers (Passeridae) are represented in the United States by only two introduced species.

**Attracting Birds**

You can encourage more birds to visit your yard by creating hospitable conditions. The most common ways to do this are to plant trees, shrubs, and flowers that birds need for food and shelter; to set up devices for dispensing food or water to birds; and to provide artificial nest boxes to attract cavity-nesting species. The setting and geographical location of your property will determine which techniques are most practical.

Planting for Birds

There are many different ways to landscape for birds, but there are several universally important considerations. Cover is especially crucial, both for nesting and for avoiding predators. By planting ground cover and low bushes beneath taller shrubs you can simulate conditions in a natural woodland. If the trees and bushes are selected carefully, their berries, fruits, and seeds will naturally attract birds. Try to select plants that produce seeds and fruit in various seasons of the year. In addition, there are many flowers that are attractive to species such as hummingbirds, or that produce seeds relished by birds.

Feeders

Birdfeeders range from the simple to the elaborate. Some of the most effective consist of plastic tubes that dispense sunflower or thistle seed from small holes on the sides.

Various finches especially like such feeders. Beef suet, which is relished by woodpeckers and nuthatches, can be suspended from tree limbs in coarsely knit bags of heavy twine. Mixed seed such as cracked corn, millet, and sunflower seed may be thrown on the ground for ground-feeders like doves and sparrows. In warm weather, feeders that hold sugar water can often replace or supplement flowers as a way to attract hummingbirds.

Baths
In all seasons, water is attractive to birds. In winter, electric coils or solar-heated baths keep water from freezing. In summer, a dripping water source is often more attractive to birds than a well-stocked birdfeeder. Whether you are offering water or food to wild birds, don't be afraid to experiment. Birds are often not as fussy as we would think.

Bird Boxes
A suitably erected bird box is often an easy way to attract cavity-nesting birds to your yard. American Kestrels, Tree Swallows, nuthatches, and wrens are all species that will readily take to a properly constructed and located bird box. Competition from House Sparrows and European Starlings may hamper nesting by native species, but with persistence you can discourage the unwanted birds.

**Bird Conservation**

Despite the great diversity of birds, many bird species are facing increasing threats to their populations. For example, in North America, certain forest-breeding birds are affected by the continuous fragmentation of large, unbroken woodlands, which heightens the exposure of the nests to predators such as cats, dogs, raccoons, and skunks. Additionally, many species that winter in Latin America are losing their tropical habitats. The combined effect has been a loss in bird populations, reflected in long-term population studies such as the Breeding Bird Survey and the National Audubon Society–Leica Christmas Bird Count.

Controlling national and international events threatening native bird populations is possible through active support of conservation legislation and local wildlife management issues. BirdLife International is an organization with global concerns for declining bird populations. So is the National Audubon Society, whose "Birds in the Balance" program is working to halt the decline of some species by identifying critical migratory stopovers and breeding grounds in North America, and wintering areas in Central and South America. Supporting groups like these is a fine way to help fill the growing need for conservation.

# THE BIRDS

## American Kestrel *Falco sparverius*

Once known as the Sparrow Hawk, this smallest of North American falcons is seen regularly in populated areas. It often perches on utility wires and poles, and in agricultural areas it hovers above the ground in search of prey. Large numbers of migrant American Kestrels may be seen, particularly along the coasts, in the spring and fall as they move to and from their more northerly breeding sites.

Identification  9–12". A small bird with relatively long, pointed wings, often seen hovering. The back and tail are rufous. The facial pattern is characterized by two black stripes. Adult males have steel-gray wings and a red tail with a black tip; females have brown wings and a brown-banded tail.

Voice  A shrill *killy killy killy.*

Habitat  Open areas, including farms, grasslands, deserts, and woodland edges.

Range  Widespread across North America, except northern Alaska and northernmost Canada. Winters throughout most of the U.S.

### California Quail  *Callipepla californica*

This large member of the pheasant family is the state bird of California. California Quail are known for forming large winter coveys of as many as several hundred birds. In spring these groups disband, as pair bonds are formed for breeding. Many a movie buff would recognize the call of the California Quail, as it can be heard in the background of many films made in California.

Identification 9–11". A chunky, gray to brown, pigeon-sized bird often found on the ground. There is a characteristic comma-shaped plume arising from the crown. Adult males have a chestnut crown, black throat, and gray chest. Underparts are scaled or streaked.

Voice A loud, nasal call, usually 3 notes, often described as *Chi-CA-go*, with emphasis on the second syllable.

Habitat Open areas with brush, chaparral; live oak canyons and suburbs, with a nearby water source.

Range California and Baja California. Introduced in the Northwest to British Columbia, Nevada, and Utah.

### Rock Dove *Columba livia*

First introduced to North America in the 17th century, the Rock Dove is known to many enthusiasts as the "homing pigeon." Rock Doves have been used at least since the days of the Roman Empire to carry messages over long distances. Their ability to return to the home roost has led ornithologists to experiment with these birds in an effort to discover how birds navigate. Although many questions still remain, it has been demonstrated that pigeons use some combination of the angle of the sun, an internal clock, and even the ability to sense the earth's magnetic fields to fix their relative position and direction of flight.

Identification  13". Typically a blue-gray bird with a white rump and a dark terminal band on the tail. There are iridescent greens and purples on the neck. Variations in overall color include brown, white, and pied forms.

Voice  A soft, mellow series of coos: *coo, coo, coo.*

Habitat  City streets, suburban parks, and bridges; also sea cliffs and canyons.

Range  Resident from southern Canada south to Mexico.

### Band-tailed Pigeon *Columba fasciata*

Although the common conception of a pigeon involves urban settings and city parks, the Band-tailed Pigeon is normally a resident of foothills, open country, and forests. Of late, however, this species has begun to join its relative the Rock Dove in suburban and even urban locales. In the wild, the Band-tailed Pigeon eats mainly acorns, but those birds that have adapted to city life feed on the berries of several kinds of ornamental plants.

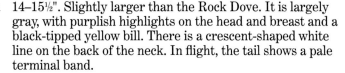

Identification 14–15½". Slightly larger than the Rock Dove. It is largely gray, with purplish highlights on the head and breast and a black-tipped yellow bill. There is a crescent-shaped white line on the back of the neck. In flight, the tail shows a pale terminal band.

Voice A repeated, two-noted cooing, low in pitch: *woo-woooh*.

Habitat Primarily mountainous regions of pine or oak; also suburban parks.

Range Western British Columbia south to California, except central California, and from Utah south to Mexico.

## Mourning Dove *Zenaida macroura*

Its stiff-winged, gliding display flight is a sure sign that the Mourning Dove is preparing to nest. These doves often carry small twigs to be used in their nests, which are typically loose saucers of sticks precariously placed on a branch. A single pair of Mourning Doves may raise as many as five broods during the nesting season. In fall and winter, large flocks of Mourning Doves are frequently found feeding in agricultural areas and weed fields.

**Identification**  11–13". Overall buff to tan, with a long, pointed tail edged in white. There is black spotting on the back and iridescent highlights on the upper breast, neck, and face. This dove's wings often make a whirring sound when the bird is flushed.

**Voice**  A melodious, mournful cooing, easily imitated: *ooh-ee-woo, woo woo, woo.*

**Habitat**  Suburbs, parks, fields, and dry uplands.

**Range**  Breeds from southern Canada south throughout the U.S. to Mexico. Regularly winters throughout the breeding range; also migrates south to Panama.

34

### Inca Dove  *Columbina inca*

An interesting adaptation in the pigeon family (which includes doves and pigeons) is the production of "milk" by the adults to feed their young. The "milk" is produced in the crop, an organ used by most birds to store food temporarily. The liquid produced is not actually milk, but rather a nutrient- and vitamin-rich fluid that is an important dietary component for recently hatched doves and pigeons. As is true of most members of the family, Inca Doves take "milk" as chicks but rely on a diet of seed for most of their lives.

Identification   7½–8". A small, ground-dwelling dove, overall grayish tan. There is a scaled look to much of the plumage. In flight, the characteristic long, white-bordered tail and rusty primaries can be seen.

Voice   A monotonous, two-noted cooing, often represented as *no hope, no hope, no hope.*

Habitat   Suburbs, ranches, cities, and fields.

Range   Southeastern California, Arizona, New Mexico, and Texas.

## **Greater Roadrunner** *Geococcyx californianus*

The facts of the Great Roadrunner's life are at least as interesting as the fictions created by the cartoon industry. The roadrunner is a ground-dwelling member of the cuckoo family. Its sizable legs and feet and massive bill help make it an efficient predator, able to run down and capture a variety of prey, including grasshoppers, scorpions, snakes, and rodents. While it is not quite the speedster of cartoon depictions, the Greater Roadrunner's agility and quickness are impressive. True to the screen, however, the Greater Roadrunner is at home in the badlands, thorn scrub, and deserts of the Southwest.

Identification 20–24". A large bird, overall dark brown with heavy streaking throughout. It has a large head with a crest, a heavy bill, and a long tail. At close range, the colorful blue and red featherless area around the eye is visible.

Voice A mournful series of coos, descending in pitch: *coo, coo, coo, coo.*

Habitat Scrub desert, mesquite groves, dry thickets, and chaparral.

Range The southwestern U.S., from California to Louisiana.

## Common Nighthawk *Chordeiles minor*

Although the Common Nighthawk's profile resembles that of a small falcon, it is a "hawk" in name only. It is a member of a largely nocturnal group of birds called nightjars. These birds all have rather large mouths encircled by specialized, bristlelike feathers. On the wing, the bird uses its basketlike mouth as an efficient insect trap. Traditionally a ground-nesting species, the Common Nighthawk also nests on flat-topped, gravel-covered roofs. Its display flights are extraordinary, accompanied by an impressive booming sound created by the wings.

Identification   8½–10". Normally observed in flight and appearing dark overall, this bird has a hawklike profile and long, pointed wings. From below, the characteristic white wing bars may be seen.

Voice   A buzzy *peee-ik*, and a *boom* like a note from a trombone.

Habitat   Open woodlands, suburbs, clearings, and fields.

Range   Breeds in most of North America, except for the Far North and the southwesternmost U.S.

## Common Poorwill *Phalaenoptilus nuttallii*

The Common Poorwill is one of the nightjars, a family whose Latin name means, roughly, "goatsuckers." It derives from an old belief that these birds sucked the milk of goats. In actuality, Common Poorwills and other members of the family are largely insect eaters. This species' common name is meant to be a phonetic representation of its call. Nightjars are persistent singers, typically beginning their performances at dusk and continuing into the night.

Identification  7–8½". A chunky, relatively small nightjar, mottled in browns and blacks with no white bars on the wings. It has short wings and a rounded tail.

Voice  A two-noted whistle, sounding like its name: *poor-will, poor-will.* The second note is higher in pitch than the first.

Habitat  Desert scrub, sagebrush, chaparral, and coniferous woodlands.

Range  Breeds in the western U.S. and British Columbia. Year-round resident in the southwesternmost states and southern Texas.

## Black-chinned Hummingbird *Archilochus alexandri*

The eastern United States has only one regularly occurring hummingbird—the Ruby-throated Hummingbird. In contrast, the West has more than a dozen different hummingbirds during the spring and summer seasons. One of the more common and widespread species is the Black-chinned Hummingbird. Male Black-chinneds are known for their spectacular swooping display flights, which can best be observed at the onset of the breeding season. The birds' tiny 1½-inch nests, constructed of plant down wrapped with spiders' webs, may be reused from year to year.

Identification  3¼–3¾". A relatively small hummingbird. Both sexes are metallic green above.Males have black chins underlined by an iridescent purplish band; females have white throats.

Voice  Buzzy chipping, trills, and wing whirring.

Habitat  Low mountain meadows, canyons, chaparral, and woodlands.

Range  From southern British Columbia south throughout the western U.S. to central Texas, except the coastal Pacific Northwest.

44

## Anna's Hummingbird *Calypte anna*

Hummingbird flight is a true marvel. Not only are these diminutive birds capable of high-speed forward flight, but they also move readily sideways or backwards or hover in midair. The relatively large flight muscles necessary to accomplish such maneuvers require an abundance of fuel. Hummingbirds must have a ready energy source, so they regularly defend their feeding territories. Anna's Hummingbird may defend a clump of fuchsias or a eucalyptus tree. This species is unusual in that it regularly spends the winter in North America.

**Identification**  3½–4". Typical hummingbird iridescent green above; the male has a rose-red crown and gorget. Females may show some red flecking on the throat. Both sexes are grayish below with some green blotching.

**Voice**  The male utters a raspy, squeaky song in flight or from a perch. Both sexes utter *chips* and *chick* calls.

**Habitat**  Gardens, brushy canyons, foothills, and oak woodlands.

**Range**  Along the West Coast from southernmost British Columbia to Baja California.

### Broad-tailed Hummingbird *Selasphorus platycerus*

The Broad-tailed is the hummingbird of the Rocky Mountains. During the summer months it may be found in the coniferous woodlands and along mountain streams below the timberline. Many hikers and birdwatchers first notice this hummer after hearing a loud, insectlike trill that is not a vocalization, but rather a sound created by air passing rapidly through the two outer primaries on the bird's wings. Only males have the specially formed feathers that result in this wing-whir. At the end of the breeding season, as the males replace flight feathers during their molt, their ability to produce the wing-whir is lost.

Identification    4–4½". Green above and white below. The male has a rose-colored gorget, and the female has pinkish flanks. The male's wing-whir is a good identifying characteristic.

Voice    A sharp *chick* call. The male has a unique wing whir.

Habitat    Mountain meadows and forests; also in gardens.

Range    The U.S. Rockies and Great Basin mountains to southern Arizona and Texas.

48

## Rufous Hummingbird *Selasphorus rufus*

Hummingbirds use energy at a rapid rate, and each foraging flight, display flight, or territorial defense flight costs them a certain amount. They have adapted by evolving several strategies for conserving energy. During the day they regularly take rests, perching quietly for a period of time. At night they actually go into a state of torpor. Body functions such as heart rate, respiration, and metabolism all slow down for several hours, reducing energy use and allowing the hummingbird to pass the night without feeding.

| | |
|---|---|
| Identification | 3–4". The male has a rufous back, tail, and sides; its gorget is metallic orange-red. Females are green above with speckled throats and rufous tails; they resemble Allen's and Broad-tailed females (see pages 52 and 48). |
| Voice | Buzzy, high-pitched *chip* notes: *chew chew chew.* |
| Habitat | Coniferous and deciduous mountain forests, lowland forests, and alpine meadows. |
| Range | The Pacific Northwest to the Alaska panhandle, inland to Montana. |

## Allen's Hummingbird  *Selasphorus sasin*

The display flights of male hummingbirds are a spectacle worth watching. Allen's Hummingbird flies back and forth, describing a large arc similar to the track of a pendulum. He then makes a series of trill-like sounds with his tail. When a female approaches, he will often hover directly in front of her or engage in a series of rapid, short flights in her general vicinity. Some hummingbirds have even been observed mating in the air. Following copulation, the male and female typically part company.

Identification  3–3½". Similar to the Rufous Hummingbird (see page 50). Males are green above with rufous underparts and tail and a red-orange gorget. Females are virtually indistinguishable from female Rufous Hummingbirds.

Voice  A series of rapid *chips* and *chups: zee chuppity chup.*

Habitat  Brush and woodlands, redwood forests, and coastal chaparral.

Range  From extreme southwestern Oregon south along the California coast.

## Acorn Woodpecker *Melanerpes formicivorus*

Within its range, the Acorn Woodpecker is a high-profile bird. Both its raucous calls and its flashy black-and-white appearance attract attention. Acorn Woodpeckers regularly create holes in trees, fence posts, and telephone poles in which they store acorns as a winter food source. During the breeding season they also eat insects. These woodpeckers form loose colonies that all use the same territories and visit the same "storage" trees. Colonies fluctuate in size from year to year, depending on the size of local supplies of acorns.

Identification 8–9½". A robin-sized woodpecker, basically black and white with a red crown. The red is restricted on the female's crown and is bordered in black. In flight, the white rump and wing patches can be seen.

Voice A noisy variety of calls, including *ja-cob, ja-cob,* and *wake-up! wake-up!*

Habitat Oak and pine-oak forests.

Range From Oregon south to Baja California, and from Arizona east to southwestern Texas.

### Red-naped Sapsucker  *Sphyrapicus nuchalis*

Three closely related species of sapsuckers occur in western North America. Ranging from west to east they are the Red-breasted Sapsucker, the Red-naped Sapsucker, and the Yellow-bellied Sapsucker. All three, in fact, were considered one species (Yellow-bellied Sapsucker) until relatively recently. Sapsuckers are woodpeckers known for their habit of drilling numerous holes in tree bark. As the sap flows, the birds eat the insects that it attracts.

Identification   8–9". A boldly patterned bird, black and white above, with a pale yellow breast. It has a red throat, chin (white in the female), crown, and patch on the back of its head, all contrasting with a black-and-white striped face. The Red-breasted Sapsucker has an all-red head and upper breast.

Voice   A down-slurred *cheer* or *wheer.*

Habitat   Mixed coniferous and deciduous forests.

Range   Summer resident of British Columbia, Washington, Oregon, and California east to the Dakotas and New Mexico. Winters in southernmost California and Arizona and south into Mexico.

## Ladder-backed Woodpecker *Picoides scalaris*

In North America, this species is restricted to the Southwest. The Ladder-backed Woodpecker resides in a number of arid habitats, including oak woodlands, mesquite brushlands, and even deserts. The Ladder-backed's diet consists mainly of caterpillars, but it also feeds on a variety of cactus fruit. The nesting season begins in late April. Typically these birds build a nest by excavating a cavity in a cactus, century plant, or deciduous tree, where the females lay between four and five eggs. Males help with incubation chores, and the chicks normally hatch in two weeks.

Identification 6–7½". As its name implies, black and white markings on this bird's upper surfaces form a ladderlike pattern. (Perhaps "zebra-backed" would be more apt.) Males have a red cap. There is a black line running from behind the eye to the ear, down the cheek, and forward toward the bill. Underparts are off-white and speckled with black.

Voice Sharp *pick!* calls and a steady rattle or whinny.

Habitat Desert scrub and dry brushlands; also towns and parks.

Range From southeastern California to central Texas.

## Downy Woodpecker *Picoides pubescens*

The Downy Woodpecker, our smallest woodpecker species, is regularly found in mixed deciduous woodlands as well as in parks and suburbs. Like other members of the woodpecker family, the Downy has evolved special structural designs of the head, tongue, and bill for excavating and extracting insect larvae from tree trunks and branches. The feet, with two toes pointing forward and two back, and proplike tail are adaptations for feeding on vertical surfaces.

Identification  6–7". A small bird, basically black above and white below. There are white areas on the back and white markings on the wings. Males have a small red crown patch. (See also Hairy Woodpecker, page 62.)

Voice  A squeaky *pick!* call and a descending whinny: *dee-dee-dee-dee-dee.*

Habitat  Mixed deciduous forests, parks, suburbs, and orchards.

Range  Resident throughout most of forested North America except in southwestern deserts.

## Hairy Woodpecker *Picoides villosus*

Like the Downy Woodpecker, the Hairy Woodpecker is widespread in North America. The Hairy, however, is less common throughout its range and seems to be relatively more restricted to extensive woodlands. Researchers have determined that woodpeckers, as they forage along a trunk or limb, may actually be able to feel and hear small wood-boring insects. After chipping through the bark, the woodpecker uses its specially adapted tongue, extruding it into the insect tunnel and retrieving the prey.

Identification    8½–10½". Similar in appearance to the Downy Woodpecker (see page 60), although larger and with a heavier bill. The outer tail feathers are entirely white in the Hairy but show black spotting in the Downy.

Voice    Call note is a squeaky *peek!*, with the *ee* sound distinguishing it from the Downy Woodpecker, whose call is *pick!;* also utters a steady, strong rattle on one pitch.

Habitat    All woodlands, from forests to suburban parks.

Range    Widespread throughout the forests of North America.

## Northern Flicker *Colaptes auratus*

The "Yellow-shafted Flicker" of the East and the "Red-shafted" and "Gilded" flickers of the West were once considered separate species. When it was realized that these groups actually consisted of one interbreeding population, these birds were reclassified as the Northern Flicker. This bird is unusual for a woodpecker: it feeds on the ground.

Identification  12½–14". Brown with black barring above; heavily spotted with black below. The western, red-shafted form has a red mustache stripe (male only) and a pale red underwing; the eastern, yellow-shafted form has a black mustache stripe (male only) and a yellow underwing. Birds in flight show a white rump patch.

Voice  A very loud *wick-wick-wick-wick-wick!* Call notes include *wicka-wicka* and a loud, down-slurred *clear!*

Habitat  Open woodlands, deserts, and suburban neighborhoods.

Range  Breeds virtually throughout North America south to Mexico; absent from southern Texas, except in winter. Found year-round in most of the U.S.

## Black Phoebe *Sayornis nigricans*

The names of some birds reflect the history of American ornithology. The Black Phoebe's generic name, *Sayornis*, means "Say's bird." Thomas Say (1787–1834) was one of the pioneering naturalists in North America. While he is perhaps best known for his insect studies, Say added much to our understanding of American birds. Black Phoebes often build their nests of mud and plant materials and under bridges. These sites provide ready access to a good supply of small, flying insects, the mainstay of the phoebe's diet.

Identification 6–7". Resembles a junco, only slightly larger. The upperparts and chest are black; the belly and undertail coverts are white. Young birds are grayish with some brown markings.

Voice An evenly paced *fee-bee, bee, bee, fee-bee, bee bee*; also a slurred *chip*.

Habitat Prefers to be near water; woodlands, suburban parks, and open chaparral.

Range From California throughout the southwesternmost states to western Texas.

66

### Say's Phoebe *Sayornis saya*

Named for Thomas Say, an early American naturalist, this is a bird of the wide-open spaces. Arid western settings are its favored haunts, and it may be found in badlands, sage flatlands, and around ranches. Like many flycatchers, it hunts from a perch, flying out to snatch a passing insect or even hovering in midair to get a better bead on its prey. At nesting time Say's Phoebe chooses a ledge or cavity in which to construct its loosely formed nest.

**Identification**  7–8". Grayish tan above, with the crown appearing rather dark. The throat and breast are mouse-gray. Perhaps the most distinctive field marks are the pinkish-tawny belly and undertail coverts.

**Voice**  A down-slurred whistle, *pee-ur,* and an ascending *preet!*

**Habitat**  Dry, sunny, open areas such as plains, canyons, and cliffs. Often near buildings.

**Range**  Breeds throughout most of the West from Alaska to Texas. Winters in the Southwest from California to southwestern Texas.

## Western Kingbird *Tyrannus verticalis*

Western Kingbirds are known for their aggressive defense of their nesting territories. Any bird that approaches the nest site will normally be "greeted" and summarily driven off. Interestingly, there are also records of Western Kingbirds nesting in the same tree with large raptors. This may be an adaptation that affords the kingbird the added protection provided by the hawk. Western Kingbirds are often observed hunting from a perch, in typical flycatcher manner. While this species is restricted to the West during the breeding season, some Western Kingbirds regularly wander to the Atlantic coast in the fall.

| | |
|---|---|
| Identification | 8–9". Upperparts, head, and chest are pale gray; the belly is lemon-yellow. There is a black tail with white outer edges. (The similar Cassin's Kingbird lacks white on its tail.) |
| Voice | A series of impulsive, rapid notes, sounding like an audiotape on fast forward. Call note is a loud *whit* or *kit*. |
| Habitat | Arid, open country; roadsides; and pastures. |
| Range | Throughout the West from southern Canada to Mexico. |

## **Tree Swallow**  *Tachycineta bicolor*

Although the swallows of Capistrano (Cliff Swallows) are better known for signaling the onset of spring, returning Tree Swallows are harbingers of the season in many areas of North America. Actually, many Tree Swallows overwinter in the extreme southern United States. While this species' summer diet consists mainly of insects, winter flocks often feed on bayberry. One of the great spectacles of fall is the enormous flocks of Tree Swallows on their way south. At times, flocks consist of hundreds of thousands of swallows.

| | |
|---|---|
| Identification | 5–6¼". A small bird, dark above and pure white below. In good light the greenish to bluish iridescent coloration on the upper surfaces is apparent. Young birds are muddy brown above and may show a faint breast band. |
| Voice | A constant, liquid twitter and chatter. |
| Habitat | Open wooded areas near marshes, ponds, or rivers. |
| Range | Breeds over most of North America, except the Far North and the southernmost states. Winters from southern California east to Florida and as far north as Long Island, New York. |

### Steller's Jay  *Cyanocitta stelleri*

Steller's Jays live up to their family's reputation for being loud and aggressive. Small flocks of these jays are regularly found in a variety of mixed and coniferous forests in western North America. Their raucous calls often herald their arrival, and they are common visitors to campsites and picnic areas. Like other jays, the Steller's Jay seems almost omnivorous and includes in its diet a variety of seeds and nuts, insects, small birds and amphibians, and even a snake or two. Steller's Jay is a talented mimic, and one vocalization is a perfect imitation for the call of the Red-tailed Hawk.

**Identification** 12–13½". The only crested jay west of the Rocky Mountains. It has a black head, throat, and upper breast and is otherwise overall dark blue.

**Voice** A grating, harsh *shack-shack-shack-shack;* also a rapid *shook-shook-shook.*

**Habitat** Coniferous and oak forests of the West.

**Range** In the West, from southern Alaska and British Columbia to extreme western Texas and Mexico.

### Scrub Jay *Aphelocoma coerulescens*

Although the range of the Scrub Jay is primarily western, there is a disjunct population in Florida. Interestingly, in this Florida population the normal pair of breeding adults is supplemented by between one and six younger birds that assist in chick-rearing. Scrub Jays in the West seem to follow the more traditional family structure, with a pair of adults raising the young. Scrub Jays are known to cache food (sometimes raiding the Acorn Woodpecker's supply), along with a variety of man-made objects, including aluminum foil, pieces of pottery, and silverware.

Identification    11–13". A large bird with a blue head (no crest), wings, and tail and a gray patch on the back. Underparts are largely gray; there is a streaked throat and a dark breast band. The Florida race has a white forehead.

Voice    A raspy *zreek!* or *jay?;* also a rapid *shook shook shook.*

Habitat    Chaparral, scrub-oak woodlands, and suburbs.

Range    In the West, from southern Washington to California and east to the Texas Hill Country. In the East, restricted to Florida.

76

### Black-billed Magpie  *Pica pica*

The two species of North American magpies are closely related to jays and crows. Within its range, the Black-billed Magpie's flashy appearance, colonial nature, and noisy vocalizations all attract attention. The magpie's success may be largely related to its ability to take advantage of a wide variety of food sources. These birds forage for insects, seeds, small rodents, and even snakes. Bold by nature, Black-billed Magpies also glean mites and ticks from deer and elk and feed regularly on road kills and the prey of carnivores.

**Identification** 17½–22". A large bird with a black head, back, and breast and a white belly. The very long tail shows green iridescence. In flight, the white wing patches are obvious.

**Voice** The song is in two parts: first a nasal, questioning *mag? mag?*; then a querulous *nag nag nag nag nag!*

**Habitat** Open range, brushlands, and farmlands.

**Range** Permanent resident from southern Alaska south through southern Nevada and east to the Dakotas and western Oklahoma.

78

### American Crow *Corvus brachyrhynchos*

There are several other crow species in North America, but the American Crow's commonly heard vocalization and widespread occurrence make it one of our more familiar birds. The American Crow has prevailed despite bounties placed on its head and indiscriminate hunting. For the birdwatcher, this crow's intricate social structures—including flock behavior, roost formation, and nesting strategies—provide a wealth of interesting opportunities for observation.

| | |
|---|---|
| Identification | 17–21". This largest North American crow species is basic black, often showing highlights. It is best identified by its voice when other crows or ravens are present. |
| Voice | A variety of calls, rattles, and clicks, the most familiar of which is the raucous *caw caw caw!* |
| Habitat | Woodlands, suburbs, city parks, and along rivers and streams lined with trees. |
| Range | Breeds throughout the southern two-thirds of Canada and most of the U.S.; absent from much of the interior Southwest. Winters south of the Canadian border. |

## Bushtit *Psaltriparus minimus*

The diminutive Bushtit is a common bird of wooded and scrub areas as well as suburbs and public gardens. Like the similar titmice and chickadees, Bushtits often forage in small flocks that regularly include kinglets, wrens, and other species, and they often nest in close association with other Bushtits. Their nest, constructed of fine plant materials and small twigs, is gourd-shaped and typically hangs beneath the branch to which it is attached. Unlike most other small songbirds, Bushtits are seldom parasitized by Brown-headed Cowbirds.

Identification 3¾–4". A small bird, basically gray above with lighter underparts. Various races and forms may show a brown cap or cheek or a black eye and cheek patch.

Voice Typical calls include a simple *tsip* or *pit;* in flocks the constant calling has a chattering or twittering quality.

Habitat Deciduous woodlands, thickets or edges, and chaparral.

Range Year-round from the Pacific Northwest south to California and east from Oregon to Texas.

### Red-breasted Nuthatch *Sitta canadensis*

Four kinds of nuthatches occur in North America. This species and the White-breasted Nuthatch (see page 86) are by far the more common and widespread. Both species regularly visit birdfeeders. Like that of other nuthatches, the Red-breasted's diet consists primarily of seeds produced by evergreen trees. In fact, the name "nuthatch" derives from the birds' practice of "hatching" or hacking open these seeds.

Identification   4½–4¾". A chickadee-sized bird that is steel-gray above with reddish to pinkish underparts. There is a black line through the eye and a white line above the eye.

Voice   A nasal *nack,* and a more rapid *anh-anh-anh,* like toots from a toy trumpet.

Habitat   Coniferous woods in summer; mixed woods on migration.

Range   Widespread in many parts of Canada and the U.S. Breeds in the West from southern Alaska and the Rockies as far south as Arizona, and in the East, from the Great Lakes and Newfoundland south in the Appalachians to North Carolina, as well as along the northeast coast.

### White-breasted Nuthatch *Sitta carolinensis*

The White-breasted Nuthatch is common and widespread across much of North America and is regularly found at birdfeeders. Like other members of its family, it can be seen foraging in its characteristic "head-first-down-the-tree" manner. This behavior may allow the nuthatch to discover insect prey overlooked by "up-the-tree" feeders such as woodpeckers and creepers. White-breasted Nuthatches nest in natural cavities, where they typically incubate between five and ten eggs. Chicks are fed a variety of insects and are attended to by both adults.

Identification    5–6". Gray above and white below. There is a black cap and variably sized areas of rust-colored feathers on the flanks, around the legs, and on the undertail coverts.

Voice    A nasal *yank-yank!*; also a rapid-fire *ank ank ank ank!* like that from a toy machine-gun.

Habitat    A wide variety of woodlands, from forests to backyards.

Range    Resident in most of southern Canada and throughout most of the U.S. except the Great Plains.

## Pygmy Nuthatch *Sitta pygmaea*

The Pygmy Nuthatch, a bird of the western coniferous forests, is the counterpart of the eastern Brown-headed Nuthatch. It often maintains year-round territories and is one of a handful of species in which cooperative breeding has been confirmed. In the Pygmy Nuthatch's case, a pair of adults is assisted by one to three helpers, usually young males. Although the adult female does all the incubating, her mate and the helpers assist with nest-building and food-gathering. Research has determined that pairs with helpers raise more young successfully than do unassisted pairs.

| | |
|---|---|
| Identification | 3¾–4½". A small bird with a characteristic gray-brown cap; otherwise, gray above and creamy below. At close range, a white smudge mark at the base of the nape may be seen. |
| Voice | A high-pitched *pee-deet, pee-deet, pee-deet*. |
| Habitat | Pine forests. |
| Range | Year-round in the interior northwestern states, extending north into British Columbia and Alberta. Elsewhere confined mainly to eastern California but seen throughout the southwestern states. |

## Cactus Wren  *Campylorhynchus brunneicapillus*

This bird is the characteristic wren of the arid Southwest. The Cactus Wren is the largest wren species in North America. As its name implies, the bird is often seen in areas where cactus grows. Its bulky nest is typically placed in a cholla or saguaro, or in a thorn tree when cactus is unavailable. Thus the vulnerable Cactus Wren chicks, surrounded by sharp spines, are afforded an extra degree of protection from predators. The nest is also used by the adult birds as a nighttime roost, as a shaded retreat, and as cover from rain.

| | |
|---|---|
| Identification | 7–8¾". A thrush-sized wren with a long bill, a brown cap, and a prominent white eye-line. It is brown above, with much white streaking and barring, and light below, with heavy spotting on the throat. |
| Voice | A harsh, scolding chatter; repetitious and unmusical. |
| Habitat | Deserts and other dry regions with cactus and mesquite. |
| Range | The extreme southwestern U.S., from California to Texas. |

### Bewick's Wren *Thryothorus bewickii*

Although still common in the western part of its range, the Bewick's Wren has decreased at an alarming rate east of the Mississippi River. The Bewick's Wren's inquisitive nature, loud and cheery song, cocked tail, and small, chunky body are typical of this family. In the West it may be found in open woodlands and brushlands, but it is also a familiar sight around residential areas, ranches, and barnyards.

Identification  5–5½". Western birds are largely gray-brown above and pale below. The upperparts of eastern birds are more rusty brown. There is a prominent white eyebrow and white markings on the outer edges of the tail.

Voice  A rather high-pitched medley of burry whistles and trills, similar to that of the Song Sparrow.

Habitat  Arid brushlands, chaparral, and woodland edges.

Range  Breeds from the Pacific Northwest south through California, the Southwest, and east to West Virginia. Winters west of the Mississippi and in the Gulf Coast states.

## House Wren *Troglodytes aedon*

During the breeding season, most bird species establish a nesting territory. This may be confined to a relatively small area directly around the nest or may range over a much larger expanse of up to several acres. The House Wren is a fitting subject for observation of a nesting territory. Both members of an established pair are quick to wreak havoc on any other House Wrens that attempt to move in. This includes direct physical attacks as well as the destruction of nests and eggs of competing pairs.

Identification  4½–5". Brownish gray above and buff below. There is a faint eyebrow and light barring on the back. The tail is often cocked in typical wren fashion.

Voice  An exuberant, cascading series of bubbling notes; also a scolding chatter, like the sound of a baby's rattle.

Habitat  Brush, woodland edges, and suburban yards.

Range  Breeds from southern Canada throughout the U.S., except in the extreme Southeast. Winters from southern California and Virginia southward.

94

### Golden-crowned Kinglet *Regulus satrapa*

The Golden-crowned Kinglet is one of our smallest birds and often associates, in small flocks, with other kinglets and chickadees. It is most at home in evergreen areas. Like some other northern species, it is known for its lack of fear of humans. It frequently approaches an observer closely and is less likely to take flight than are other small songbirds.

Identification    3¼–4". A tiny bird, overall olive-green above and light gray below. There is a white eyebrow and white wingbars. The brilliantly colored crown, gold in males and yellow in females, is not always apparent unless the bird is displaying.

Voice    A very high-pitched, thin *see-see-see-see,* ending with chickadee-like chatter.

Habitat    Coniferous forests.

Range    Breeds from Alaska to Newfoundland, south in suitable coniferous forests in California, Colorado, Minnesota, and the southern Appalachians; absent from the Great Plains and most of the Southeast. Winters from southern Canada throughout most of the U.S.

96

### Ruby-crowned Kinglet *Regulus calendula*

The tiny Ruby-crowned Kinglet seems to be in almost constant motion. Often, just as a birdwatcher focuses on it, the bird flits off to another location. Fortunately, these birds normally forage in one tree long enough for an observer to relocate them. Ruby-crowneds frequently feed on insects at the tips of branches. For small birds they have a big voice.

Identification
: 3¾–4½". A small bird, olive-gray above and pale lemon-yellow below, with white wingbars and eye-ring. This species lacks the striped crown of the Golden-crowned Kinglet.

Voice
: A series of very high, thin notes, *see see see see,* bursting into a rolling bubble, *chubby-chubby-tee-chah!* Calls include a scolding *ji-dit, ji-dit.*

Habitat
: Coniferous forests in summer; coniferous and mixed woodlands and thickets in winter.

Range
: Breeds from northwestern Alaska and Newfoundland, south in the mountains to Baja California, New Mexico, the Great Lakes region, and northern New England. Winters from British Columbia, northern Texas, and Maryland south.

98

## Western Bluebird *Sialia mexicana*

The three species of North American bluebirds are all noted for their magnificent plumage, musical songs, and regular occurrence around human habitations. Unfortunately, all three species have suffered significant declines during the 20th century. Like the Western Bluebird, the others are cavity nesters. As dead trees and snags are cleared, many suitable nesting sites are eliminated.

**Identification** 6–7". Slightly smaller than a robin, this bird has a deep blue hood and upperparts. Below, there are rust-colored feathers on the chest and a light gray belly. Females are gray-brown above and generally show less vibrant colors.

**Voice** A soft warble, interspersed with a soft call note, *few*.

**Habitat** Woodland edges, meadows, and open areas studded with trees; also at high elevations.

**Range** Breeds from southern British Columbia and Montana south to Baja California and extreme western Texas. Retreats from its northern breeding range in winter, with birds overwintering in the southwestern U.S.

## Swainson's Thrush *Catharus ustulatus*

The spot-breasted thrushes are not as brilliantly colored as their close relatives the bluebirds, but they make up for that with their ethereal voices. Their flutelike song is heard in damp coniferous areas. Like many songbirds that spend the winter in Central and South America, the Swainson's Thrush makes perilous journeys. Each year hundreds are killed during their nocturnal travels when they collide with radio towers and other tall, man-made structures.

**Identification** 6½-7¾". Slightly smaller than a robin. Five North American species are similar, being brownish to olive above and light below, with varying amounts of spotting on the chest and flanks. The Swainson's Thrush has a buff eye-ring.

**Voice** A series of upward-spiraling, flutelike phrases. Call note is a repeated *whit, whit*.

**Habitat** Northern coniferous forests, mountain thickets, and swamps.

**Range** Breeds from central Alaska to Newfoundland south to California and New Mexico, the Great Lakes, and West Virginia.

102

### Hermit Thrush *Catharus guttatus*

The four species of spot-breasted thrushes occurring in the West look similar, but the Hermit Thrush can often be identified by its habit of slowly raising and lowering its tail after it has settled on a perch. Its haunting, flutelike vocalization has earned it the nicknames "American nightingale" and "swamp angel."

**Identification**  6½–8". Slightly smaller than a robin. Five North American species are similar, being brownish to olive above and light below, with varying amounts of spotting on the chest and flanks. The Hermit Thrush is distinguished by its rufous tail; it also has a white eye-ring.

**Voice**  A series of flutelike phrases, beginning with a long, lower note and rising in a higher tremolo. Call notes include a single whine, like that of a harmonica, and a low *chuck*.

**Habitat**  Coniferous forests and mixed woodlands.

**Range**  Breeds from central Alaska to Newfoundland south to California and New Mexico, the Great Lakes, and West Virginia. Winters on the West Coast and in the southern U.S. as far north as New Jersey.

## American Robin *Turdus migratorius*

Perhaps our best-known songbird, the American Robin occurs throughout North America during the breeding season. Its arrival is considered a sure sign of spring in many areas, but this species actually overwinters in most of the contiguous 48 states. Their singsong vocalization, however, does signify the beginning of their nesting season. Robins are often observed on suburban lawns, cocking their heads as if listening for prey. In actuality, American Robins rely solely on sight to capture worms.

Identification   9–11". Gray-brown above; orange to rust-red below. There is a yellow bill and white marks around the eye and on the throat. Immatures are heavily spotted below.

Voice   The phrases of the robin's well-known song rise and fall in pitch: *cheerily-cheer-up! cheerily-cheer-up!* Call notes include a whinny, a *chuck,* and *tut, tut.*

Habitat   Neighborhoods, suburban parks, and woodlands.

Range   Breeds throughout most of North America south to Mexico. Winters mainly in the southern two-thirds of the U.S.

**Varied Thrush** *Ixoreus naevius*

While many bird species make epic migrations twice a year, others are year-round residents in one locale. Still other species undergo rather limited seasonal movements. The Varied Thrushes summering in the northern part of their range move southward to the Northwest and California to spend the winter. Other Varied Thrushes, breeding around mountain lakes in the Northwest and California, simply retreat to the lowlands. A few are reported as far east as the Atlantic coast each year.

Identification 9–10". Similar to the American Robin. Blue-gray (males) or brown (females) above and rust-orange below. There is an orange eyebrow and wingbars, as well as a black (gray in females) breast band.

Voice Whistles a slow song of 2 or 3 buzzy notes, with a definite interval following each note. Call note is a soft *took*.

Habitat Dense, moist, coniferous or deciduous forests.

Range Breeds from Alaska south to Oregon and northern California. Winters in the Pacific Northwest and California.

## Wrentit *Chamaea fasciata*

Named for its features, which seem to combine the head and bill of a titmouse and the cocked tail of a wren, the Wrentit actually seems to have no close relatives; it is the sole member of its family. The Wrentit occupies a relatively small territory of approximately two and a half acres for its entire adult life. Open spaces and rivers appear to present boundaries that Wrentits are loathe to cross. These birds also form lifelong pair bonds, with both sexes singing in an apparent continuing proclamation of their territory.

Identification  6–6½". Basically brown, but birds in the southern portions of their range are grayish brown with conspicuous white or cream-colored eyes. The long tail is sometimes cocked. The Wrentit's presence is frequently indicated by its song.

Voice  An accelerating trill beginning with a few single notes: *peep peep peep-pep-pep-prprprrr.* Call is a creaky *krr krr krr krr.*

Habitat  Chaparral, coniferous brush, and shrubs.

Range  Coastal Oregon, California, and south to Baja California.

## Northern Mockingbird *Mimus polyglottos*

Some birds are very secretive, while others seem to make an art out of display. The Northern Mockingbird definitely belongs to the latter group. Because they regularly establish and defend their wintering as well as breeding territories, mockingbirds spend much of their time proclaiming their space, both vocally and visually. One of the delights of birdwatching (and listening) is developing a catalog of the various sounds of a local Northern Mockingbird.

Identification 9–11". Overall gray, darker above and lighter below. In flight, the flashy white wing patches may be seen. This bird often perches conspicuously on an exposed branch, telephone pole, or chimney pipe.

Voice An emphatic and tireless singer, this bird mimics the songs of other birds, repeating phrases usually 3 or more times. Call note is a harsh *tchak*.

Habitat Yards, thickets, scrub, and woodland edges.

Range More or less resident from California, Wisconsin, and Nova Scotia south to Mexico and Florida.

112

## Curve-billed Thrasher *Toxostoma curvirostre*

The Mimidae, or mockingbird family, is sometimes referred to as the mimic thrush family. It includes such birds as catbirds, mockingbirds, and thrashers. All members of the family have relatively complex songs, and some are excellent mimics. The Curve-billed Thrasher is one of four grayish western thrashers with long, down-curved bills. Of the four, this species is the most widespread and occurs as far east as central Texas. Typical of its family, the Curve-billed Thrasher often selects a conspicuous perch from which to sing his elaborate song.

Identification    9½–11½". Similar in size and shape to the Northern Mockingbird (see page 112) but brownish with a mottled upper breast and a long, down-curved bill.

Voice    A complex mix of trills, warbles, and whiny notes. Call is a sharp 2- or 3-note *whit-wheet!* or *whit-wheet-wheet!*

Habitat    Cactus deserts and semiarid brushlands of the Southwest.

Range    Arizona, New Mexico, southern Colorado, and eastern and southern Texas.

## California Thrasher *Toxostoma redivivum*

This is another of the long-billed, grayish-brown thrashers of western North America (see Curve-billed Thrasher, page 114), but the California Thrasher is restricted to that state, where it is regularly found around human habitations. The California Thrasher spends much of its time foraging beneath fallen leaves for insects. In fact, it seems disinclined to fly unless forced to. This thrasher's repertoire includes songs of the Red-tailed Hawk, the California Quail, and the House Finch, as well as the non-avian sounds of frogs and even of coyotes.

| | |
|---|---|
| Identification | 11–13". Dark gray-brown above with a long, down-curved bill. The belly and undertail coverts are cinnamon-buff. A pale eyebrow is apparent. |
| Voice | Like other mimics, this bird sings long, complicated renditions of other species' songs, repeating phrases once or twice. Call is a low, harsh *cheik*. |
| Habitat | Chaparral, foothills, brushy parks, and gardens. |
| Range | Year-round resident of California, west of the Sierra Nevada and south to northern Baja California. |

## Cedar Waxwing *Bombycilla cedrorum*

Cedar Waxwings derive their common name from their preference for cedar berries and from the waxy red secretions at the ends of their secondary wing feathers. They are gregarious wanderers whose movements, especially in winter, are governed by their search for concentrations of small fruits and berries. In summer, they also feed like flycatchers on flying insects.

**Identification** 6½–8". Upperparts and breast are warm brown; belly is yellowish. The black face mask, crested head, and yellow terminal band on the gray tail are most distinctive; there are also red tips to the secondaries. Juveniles are duller.

**Voice** A high, lisping *ssseee* or *tseee tseeetseee*.

**Habitat** Residential areas, roadsides, woodland edges, and orchards; usually near berries or fruit trees.

**Range** Breeds from southern Alaska to Newfoundland, south to northern California, Virginia, and in the mountains to Georgia. Winters throughout most of the U.S.; absent from high mountains.

118

## Phainopepla *Phainopepla nitens*

The Phainopepla is the only North American member of the silky flycatcher family, a group of birds found mostly in the tropics. Closely related to waxwings, Phainopeplas share the waxwings' fondness for insects and berries. Also like the waxwings, they frequently travel in nomadic groups in search of ripe berries. The male assumes most of the nest-building chores.

**Identification**  7–7¾". Males are shiny black with a characteristic crest and red eyes. Females and young birds are gray. There are flashy wing patches, white in the males and pale gray in females and juveniles.

**Voice**  Common calls include an up-slurred, whistled *hoooeet* and a low *quirk*. The seldom-heard song is a sweet warble.

**Habitat**  Birds nest early in spring in mesquite country along watercourses, where they feed on mistletoe berries and insects. In late spring they move to a wetter, cooler habitat, where a second nesting occurs.

**Range**  Central California and the extreme southwestern states to westernmost Texas.

120

## European Starling *Sturnus vulgaris*

For the urban birdwatcher, the aerial gyrations of starlings going to roost at twilight beneath traffic-crowded bridges provide a daily pleasure. In addition, starlings are skillful mimics and exhibit a number of other engaging behaviors that are readily observable. Unfortunately, since their introduction into the United States from Europe in the late 1800s, they have become serious city and agricultural pests. Their cavity-nesting behavior is frequently at the expense of native hole-nesting species.

Identification 7½–8½". A chunky bird with a short, square tail. In spring, it is black with an iridescent blue-and-green gloss and a yellow bill. Winter plumage is heavily speckled with white. Juveniles are dusky gray.

Voice A remarkable variety of chatters, squeaks, clicks, and whistles; often gives a "wolf whistle," as well as mimicking other birds.

Habitat Cities, parks, roadsides, coastal salt marshes, and farmland.

Range Throughout the U.S. and southern Canada.

## Warbling Vireo  *Vireo gilvus*

Vireos are similar in size and behavior to New World warblers, a group with which they are often confused by inexperienced birdwatchers. In general, vireos are somewhat more sluggish in their movements than warblers, and their bills are relatively thicker and stubbier. Whereas some vireos are brightly marked with yellow, the Warbling Vireo is drab to a fault. It spends the majority of its time in the heavily foliaged canopy, so the birdwatcher should become familiar with its song. Warbling Vireos are known for their fondness for streamside woodlands as well as for the shade trees of the suburbs.

Identification | 4½–5½". Grayish-green above, pale below, and lacking wingbars. There is a dark line behind the eye. The flanks may show a pale yellow wash.

Voice | A sweet, evenly paced warble with regular up and down phrasing. Call note is a whiny *tway tway*.

Habitat | Deciduous and mixed woods.

Range | Common throughout the woodlands of North America from Canada to Mexico.

124

## Orange-crowned Warbler *Vermivora celata*

The Orange-crowned may be the most common and widespread warbler of the West. Like the Warbling Vireo (see page 124), however, it is distinguished by its lack of distinguishing features. The fact that the bird is named "Orange-crowned" would seem to indicate a suitable field mark, but this mark is only rarely seen in the field and is absent in juvenile birds.

Identification   4½–5½". A plain bird, lacking wingbars, eye-ring, or other bold field marks. Color is olive-gray but with yellow undertail coverts. Birds may show faint streaking on the sides of the breast and the flanks.

Voice   A staccato trill going up or down the scale at the end of each song. Call is a sharp *stick*.

Habitat   Thickets, brushy clearings, and forest edges.

Range   Breeds from Alaska throughout Canada to Labrador and Quebec, and throughout the western U.S. west of the Dakotas. Winters in the southern U.S.

## Yellow Warbler *Dendroica petechia*

Some birders consider warblers the butterflies of the feathered world. Approximately four dozen species of wood warblers are summer residents of North America. Their diverse plumages and interesting songs are a challenge and delight to North American bird enthusiasts. The Yellow Warbler is one of our more common species, and nesting pairs can be found throughout the states except in the Deep South. Cowbirds pose a potential threat to Yellow Warblers. These nest parasites lay their eggs in the warblers' nests, often at the expense of their unknowing hosts.

Identification    4½–5¼". A sparrow-sized bird that is largely yellow with darker wing feathers and rusty streaks on the male's chest.

Voice    A clear, loud, whistled *sweet, sweet, sweet! Sweeter than sweet!* Call note is a down-slurred *cheep*.

Habitat    Brushy thickets near water, edges of woodlands, and suburban parks.

Range    Breeds from Alaska throughout most of Canada and the U.S. Winters in the tropics.

## Yellow-rumped Warbler  *Dendroica coronata*

The western race of this species was formerly known as
Audubon's Warbler and was distinguished from the eastern
Myrtle Warbler. Because these birds are now known to
consist of a single interbreeding population, ornithologists
have redefined the two entities as one species. There are
plumage differences, however (see below). In the West, the
Yellow-rumped may nest high in the mountains.

Identification 5–6". Overall gray to black with a white belly. There is a
characteristic yellow rump and, in western birds, a yellow
throat. Yellow marks may also be obvious on the sides and
crown. Juveniles are brownish above and streaked below.

Voice A soft, loosely spaced trill followed by a jumble of notes at
the end. Call note is a *chep, chep.*

Habitat Coniferous forests during breeding season; in other seasons,
any woodlands.

Range Breeds in the boreal forests from Alaska to Newfoundland
and the western states, and year-round on the West Coast.
Winters across the southern U.S. and in Baja California
and Mexico.

## Common Yellowthroat *Geothlypis trichas*

Like people, individual birds and birds from different geographical areas often have distinct accents or dialects. The Common Yellowthroat's song, the familiar *witchity-witchity-witchity*, may vary from bird to bird or region to region. At times the basic phrase may sound like *witchity*, at other times like *witchy*, or even like *witchery*. Its loud, distinctive call note is also an excellent aid to identifying an unseen bird in heavy cover.

Identification 4½–6". A sparrow-sized bird. Both sexes are olive above and yellow (varying regionally from bright to pale) below. Adult males are readily recognized by their bold, black face masks; females are less distinctive but are normally identifiable by their plain olive and yellow plumage.

Voice Variable. A loud, rolling *witchity-witchity-witchity*, often repeated. Call note is a dry *tchet*.

Habitat Moist woodlands, thickets, marshes, and swamps.

Range Breeds throughout most of North America. Winters north to central California and South Carolina.

132

## Yellow-breasted Chat  *Icteria virens*

Although this bird's physical characteristics and behavior seem quite different from those of the typical warbler, it is nonetheless classified with that group. The Yellow-breasted Chat seems to lead two lives. At times a high-profile character, given to elaborate flight displays and wondrously complex vocalizations, the chat is at other times quite bashful, failing to utter a single peep or move from its place of cover in a dense thicket. The Yellow-breasted Chat shares with its warbler relatives a fondness for insects, and it also eats a variety of wild berries and grapes.

Identification  6½–7½". A relatively large bird, dark olive above, with a conspicuous yellow throat and chest and a white belly. There is a heavy bill and white spectacles.

Voice  A disjointed, elaborate mix of loud shrieks, whistles, rattles, and squawks, often sung from a perch or in flight.

Habitat  Streamside thickets and dense shrubs.

Range  Breeds from coast to coast in the U.S. except central and southern Florida.

## Western Tanager *Piranga ludoviciana*

More than 200 species of tanagers occur in the Western Hemisphere. A majority are tropical, and only five species range north to temperate North America. The Western Tanager, regularly found in coniferous areas of the West, summers farther north than any other tanager. While its colorful plumage is typical of its family, the melodious song is somewhat unusual among tanagers, many of which are rated as poor singers or have no song at all. Breeding pairs of Western Tanagers share chick-rearing responsibilities.

Identification   6–7½". The male in breeding plumage has a striking red head and a yellow body. Wings and tail are black. There are also yellow wingbars. Females and young are olive-green above and yellow below.

Voice   A robinlike singsong but with a burry quality to the tone. Call note is a distinctive *pri-di-dic*.

Habitat   Open coniferous and mixed forests.

Range   Breeds in western North America from the Alaskan panhandle to Saskatchewan and south to New Mexico, skirting the deserts.

136

## Black-headed Grosbeak *Pheucticus melanocephalus*

The Black-headed Grosbeak is a member of the finch family, the largest family of North American birds. This species is fairly common throughout the West and is the counterpart of the eastern Rose-breasted Grosbeak. The Black-headed Grosbeak's large bill is ideally suited for seed-cracking, but these birds also take a variety of berries and insects.

**Identification**  6½–7¾". Adult males are black above with an orange collar and breast and extensive white areas on the wings. Females are brown above, finely streaked with black and tan below. Females and juveniles have a masklike face pattern. In flight, the yellow wing linings are shown.

**Voice**  A long, melodious song sung from a high perch, similar to a robin's but richer in tone, with a singsong quality. Call note is a sharp *ik!* or *spik!*

**Habitat**  Forest edges, orchards, and gardens.

**Range**  A western bird. From southern British Columbia and extreme southern Saskatchewan and as far east as the Great Plains, south to its wintering grounds in Mexico.

## Lazuli Bunting *Passerina amoena*

Like the grosbeaks (see Black-headed Grosbeak, page 138), this species and its eastern counterpart, the Indigo Bunting, are close relatives, with some hybridization occurring between the two. At boundary areas even their songs are similar: One species often incorporates phrases from the other's "normal" repertoire. Lazuli Buntings occupy a range of habitats from desert badlands to sage flats to wooded valleys.

**Identification**  5–5½". Males are largely blue above, including the chin and throat, with white wingbars. There is a characteristic cinnamon-buff area on the lower chest and a white belly. Females are largely buff-colored above with bluish rumps.

**Voice**  A relatively fast, high-pitched jumble of notes, falling in pitch toward the end, with some of the phrases paired. Call note is a buzzy *zzzd*.

**Habitat**  Streamside brushland and edges of deciduous and mixed woods, as well as chaparral.

**Range**  Southern British Columbia, Manitoba, and Saskatchewan, south to California and northern Oklahoma.

### Rufous-sided Towhee *Pipilo erythrophthalmus*

This widespread, oversized sparrow relative is a conspicuous bird that scratches in the leaves of undergrowth and forest clearings. Being ground-nesters, towhees may be declining due to an increase in ground predators such as cats and raccoons, as well as because of steady forest regeneration of previously abandoned brushy pastures.

Identification  7–8½". Western male has a black head and throat; the upperparts are black, heavily spotted with white; and the breast and belly are white, bordered by rufous sides and flanks. White spots in the wings and outer tail feathers are seen in flight. Areas that are black in the male are brown in the female.

Voice  Variable. At times trill-like, or *chup-chup-zeeeee.*

Habitat  Forest edges and clearings, brushy areas, pine barrens, and parks with shrubby undergrowth.

Range  Breeds from southern British Columbia to Maine, south to Mexico and Florida; absent from most of the Great Plains. Winters throughout the southern two-thirds of the U.S.

## California Towhee *Pipilo crissalis*

Towhees are members of the finch family and are closely related to the sparrows. Because they spend much of their time on the ground in brushy areas, towhees are fairly easy to overlook. Ornithologists have recently split the entity formerly known as the Brown Towhee into two separate species, known respectively as the California Towhee and the Canyon Towhee. This was largely the result of researchers' observations that the vocalizations and the behavior of the coastal California Towhee are different from those of the interior Canyon Towhee.

**Identification** 8–10". A rather plain bird, overall earth-colored but somewhat lighter below. There is a faint necklace and rust-colored undertail coverts. The Canyon Towhee has a rust-colored crown and a dark central breast spot.

**Voice** Similar notes repeated in an accelerating rhythm. Call note is a sharp, metallic *chink*.

**Habitat** Chaparral foothills, brushlands, and suburban gardens.

**Range** Permanent resident of Oregon and California and south through Baja California.

144

## Lark Sparrow *Chondestes grammacus*

These ground-dwelling sparrows, known for their sociability, regularly gather in small flocks to feed in winter and even during the nesting season. Whereas pairs seem to be the norm, with males and females choosing the nest site together, a single male will sometimes court and mate with two females.

Identification 5½–6¾". Both the head and tail patterns are distinctive. The chestnut facial patches outlined in white and black give a masked appearance. The rounded tail is dark in the center and boldly bordered with white. There is also a black spot on the plain gray chest.

Voice A complex variety of repeated trills, whistles, and buzzes, interspersed with a rapid *chow-chow-chow.* Call note is *tsip.*

Habitat Dry fields, farmlands, and open woodlands.

Range In Canada from southernmost British Columbia to Manitoba, and in the U.S. from the West Coast as far east as Virginia. Winters in the southernmost parts of its range, and along the Pacific, southern Atlantic, and Gulf coasts.

### Black-throated Sparrow  *Amphispiza bilineata*

Nicknamed the "desert sparrow," this species is well adapted to life in the arid deserts, sage flats, and brushlands of the southwestern United States. While it visits waterholes and other water sources when they are available, like many desert animals it is capable of satisfying its water requirements from the liquids in the insects and vegetation it eats. In spring, Black-throated Sparrows build their cuplike nests in shrubby thickets and lay two to four pale blue eggs that hatch in approximately two weeks. In winter, they often feed with other sparrows in mixed flocks.

Identification    4¾–5½". Dusky above and lighter below. Adults have a characteristic dark cheek and a diamond-shaped black bib on the chin, throat, and upper breast. There is a white eyebrow and mustache stripe.

Voice    A musical song consisting of a few clear, introductory notes and ending with a trill.

Habitat    Deserts.

Range    Year-round resident of the southwestern U.S. Breeding range extends north to Nevada and Utah.

### Fox Sparrow *Passerella eliaca*

Tropical deforestation is often mentioned prominently as a reason for the decline of North American songbirds. Fox Sparrows do not winter in the tropics, but they have declined as well. Fragmentation of forest nesting areas and degradation of wintering sites may be the culprits.

Identification 6–7¼". A relatively large sparrow with a large bill. Many are chocolate to fox-colored red above with heavily streaked underparts. Birds in the Rockies tend to be paler, while those on the Pacific coast are dark brown. The heads and backs of birds of the westernmost mountains are gray.

Voice Phrases consist of several short, clear or burry whistles on different pitches, ending in a trill. Call is a sharp *tich tich.*

Habitat Thickets and undergrowth of coniferous or mixed forests, and chaparral.

Range Breeds in the Far North from Alaska to Newfoundland, and in the western U.S. south to California and Colorado. Winters in the Pacific Northwest to central California and across most of the southern U.S. to Georgia, and as far north as Massachusetts.

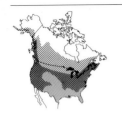

### Song Sparrow *Melospiza melodia*

The Song Sparrow is one of the most common songbirds in North America. Although modest in plumage, it has a cheery and highly variable song that is a characteristic early spring sound. In flight, the Song Sparrow typically pumps its rather long, rounded tail as it skips from one patch of cover to another. There is wide geographical variation in this species.

| | |
|---|---|
| Identification | 5–7". Most are brown above and streaked with gray and black. The underparts are whitish, heavily streaked with brown. There is a broad gray stripe above the eye and a wide dark stripe on each side of the throat. |
| Voice | Song is highly variable, typically beginning with several clear notes, *sweet sweet sweet,* followed by a jumbled trill and falling in pitch. Call note is a distinctive *chimp.* |
| Habitat | Fields, meadows, and woodland edges. |
| Range | Breeds from southern Alaska to Newfoundland, south to New Mexico, northwestern Kansas, northern Georgia, and South Carolina. Winters from the southern half of its breeding range to Florida and Mexico. |

### White-crowned Sparrow  *Zonotrichia leucophrys*

The White-crowned Sparrow is another of the western finches that show a considerable amount of geographic variation. White-crowned Sparrows breeding in the western mountains and Arctic tundra have black lores (the areas in front of the eyes). Birds from Alaska east to Hudson Bay have white or gray lores and smaller bills. White-crowned Sparrows along the Pacific coast are browner overall and have whitish lores. Because White-crowned Sparrows are migratory, westerners may see each of these forms.

Identification  7". A relatively large sparrow that often looks big-headed. It has a black-and-white striped head and a gray breast. Bill color varies from pink to orange. Young birds are heavily streaked below. (See also the variations described above.)

Voice  A series of clear and burry whistles, varying in pitch and ending in a trill. Call is a *pink, pink* and a thin *tseep.*

Habitat  Forest edges, brushy areas and thickets, and gardens.

Range  Breeds in the Far North and in the western U.S. Winters in most of the southern U.S., except the extreme Southeast.

## Dark-eyed Junco *Junco hyemalis*

Juncos, or "snowbirds," are best known as ground-feeding winter patrons of suburban birdfeeders. Their nervous behavior, flashing white outer tail feathers, and twittering call notes make them easy to distinguish whether they are encountered in a winter landscape or in the mountainous or northern coniferous forests that are their summer home.

Identification
5–6½". A bird of several distinct western forms. The "Oregon" race has a black (in males) or brown (in females) hood and a brown mantle, the flanks are buff, and the belly and outer tail feathers are white. The "White-winged" form of the Black Hills is gray above with white wingbars. The "Gray-headed" form of the Southwest is largely pale gray with a rufous back. Both sexes normally have pink bills.

Voice
A loose trill, usually on one pitch. Calls include a rapid twittering, and a dull smacking sound.

Habitat
Woodlands, fields, and brushy areas; suburban yards in winter.

Range
Breeds throughout the West from Alaska to Arizona and New Mexico. Winters in the extreme Southwest.

156

## Red-winged Blackbird *Agelaius phoeniceus*

This species is perhaps our best-known wetland bird. Its spring arrival is anticipated by birders in many parts of the country. Flocks of males arrive first and stake claim to their summer breeding territories. Their advertising song is frequently heard at this time. Females soon follow, and nesting proceeds throughout the summer. In fall, large flocks of blackbirds regularly canvass agricultural areas in search of unharvested seed.

| | |
|---|---|
| Identification | 7–9½". Males are distinctive, being black with red shoulder patches; at times these patches are well hidden. Females look more sparrowlike, largely brown and heavily streaked. Both have the long, pointed bill typical of blackbirds. |
| Voice | A robust, conspicuous *konk-a-ree!* |
| Habitat | Marshes, swamps, meadows, and pastures. |
| Range | Breeds from southern Alaska, southern Ontario, and Newfoundland south throughout the U.S. Winters in much of the southern two-thirds of the U.S. and the temperate Northwest. |

### Western Meadowlark *Sturnella neglecta*

The two meadowlark species occurring in North America are members of the blackbird family. Because the Eastern Meadowlark was so well known by early New World naturalists, the initial explorers of the American West assumed that the look-alike bird they found west of the Mississippi was the same species. Thus John J. Audubon gave it the Latin name *neglecta*. He noted, however, that Lewis and Clark had been aware that the bird had a different song than its eastern counterpart.

Identification 8½–11". A chunky field bird looking somewhat like a large sparrow, overall tan above with much streaking. There are, however, a yellow chin and breast and a black bib. In flight, the white outer tail feathers are characteristic.

Voice A melodious song of flutelike whistles; some of the notes have a gurgling quality. Call note is a low *chup*.

Habitat Grasslands, open farmlands, and prairies.

Range From the prairie provinces of western Canada south through the western U.S. and into the Midwest.

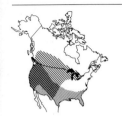

## Brewer's Blackbird *Euphagus cyanocephalus*

A variety of species known commonly as blackbirds occur across North America. Brewer's Blackbird is one of the typical western blackbirds. Because they take advantage of agricultural endeavors, these birds are regularly found on ranches and farms and even in suburban gardens. In fact, it was the spread of agriculture across the West that encouraged the expansion of Brewer's Blackbird eastward. These birds are highly social; during the breeding season they may nest in colonies of up to 100 pairs.

Identification 8–10". The breeding-plumaged male has a glossy purplish head, glossy deep green body, and characteristic yellow eyes. Females are gray-brown with dark eyes. In fall, males may have a barred, rather rusty appearance.

Voice A harsh, creaking *ksh-ee*, rising in pitch on the *ee*. Call note is a *check*.

Habitat Agricultural areas, grasslands, roadsides, and towns.

Range Breeds from British Columbia east to the Great Lakes in the North, and in the West south to New Mexico. Winters in the southern half of the U.S.

162

### Great-tailed Grackle *Quiscalus mexicanus*

The three species of North American grackles may be recognized by their long, keel-shaped tails. The Great-tailed Grackle is the largest of the three. During the nesting season the male will pose on an exposed perch, with body feathers fluffed out and tail and wings extended. After noisily ruffling his feathers, he utters a series of loud vocalizations and then points his bill skyward, apparently well pleased with his efforts.

Identification  12–17". A large bird. Males are overall greenish black with a purplish gloss on the head, back, and chest and a long, keel-shaped tail. Females are overall cinnamon-brown with dark barring below. Westernmost females are smaller and paler. Adults have bright to pale yellow eyes; juveniles, dark eyes.

Voice  A raucous mix of squeals, whistles, and rapid-fire *chucks;* also a harsh *chack.*

Habitat  Wetlands, town parks, and open lands with tall trees.

Range  In the southwestern U.S. from extreme southwestern California to Louisiana, and as far north as Nebraska during the breeding season.

164

### Brown-headed Cowbird *Molothrus ater*

Formerly confined to prairie grasslands, where they foraged at the feet of grazing bison, cowbirds gradually spread eastward and westward as land was cleared for agriculture and timber. Today they increasingly represent a threat to songbirds, which they parasitize by laying their eggs in the smaller birds' nests. Considering that a single female cowbird may lay up to 20 eggs, it is not surprising that cowbirds are thought to be seriously jeopardizing the breeding success of several species.

Identification   6–8". The adult male is glossy black with a rich brown head; the female is smaller and uniformly brownish gray. Juveniles are pale gray with indistinct streaks below. This species' bill is thick and finchlike. Southwestern birds are smaller than their eastern counterparts.

Voice   A squeaky, bubbly song. Female gives dry chatter.

Habitat   Farmlands, fields, open woodlands, and suburbs.

Range   Breeds from southern British Columbia, northern Alberta, and Nova Scotia south throughout most of southern Canada and the U.S.

## Northern Oriole *Icterus galbula*

Orioles are members of the blackbird, or troupial, family. The word troupial is derived from the birds' habit of gathering in troops or large flocks. Northern Orioles, however, typically display such behavior only on their wintering grounds. This is another species that has two distinct North American forms: the "Baltimore Oriole" in the East and the "Bullock's Oriole" in the West.

Identification
7–8½". The male of the western, or Bullock's, form is black above with a black crown and eye-stripe, mantle, and central tail feathers; below it is largely orange with a black throat. There is a white wing patch. The female is olive-gray with a yellow throat and a white belly.

Voice
A jumbled, rich whistle, sung on a variety of pitches; also a distinctive, warning chatter.

Habitat
A variety of open woodlands, suburban parks, and overgrown orchards.

Range
The Bullock's form occurs in the western half of Canada and the U.S. and south through Texas. In the Great Plains it overlaps the Baltimore form.

### Scott's Oriole  *Icterus parisorum*

This oriole is restricted to the western United States, occurring in arid portions of the Southwest. Scott's Orioles leave their southerly wintering grounds in early April. Typically the males arrive first and claim nesting territories. As females move north, breeding pairs are established, and both birds participate in the songs that will maintain the pair bond. The Scott's Oriole's intricately woven nest normally holds from two to four eggs. Chicks hatch after approximately two weeks of incubation and fledge the nest two weeks after hatching.

Identification  7½–8¼". The male is lemon-yellow with a black tail, hood (extending down the upper back, throat, and upper breast), and wings. The female is duller yellow with dark streaking on the head, back, and throat.

Voice  A rich medley of whistles. Call note is a harsh *chuck*.

Habitat  Semidesert woodlands.

Range  Summers in the southwestern U.S., from southern California to central Texas.

**Purple Finch** *Carpodacus purpureus*

Purple Finches regularly attend birdfeeders in winter, although their numbers are highly variable from season to season. In this species, first-year males resemble females, thus giving the false impression that females sing. Most often the best clue to the presence of Purple Finches is the soft *tic* call notes.

Identification 5¼–6". The adult male is raspberry-red on the head, back, rump, throat, and breast; the belly and undertail coverts are white; the flanks are indistinctly streaked with brown. Females and immatures are heavily streaked with brown.

Voice A rich, bubbly outburst of rapidly delivered notes on various pitches; some notes in pairs. Call note is a dry *tic* or *pick.*

Habitat Coniferous and mixed forests and well-planted residential areas; feeders in winter.

Range Breeds from British Columbia to Newfoundland, south in the West to southern California; also from the north-central U.S. to the Atlantic coast, south in Appalachians to Virginia. Winters from southern Canada irregularly south to Mexico and the Gulf Coast.

172

## Cassin's Finch *Carpodacus cassinii*

Closely related birds are often separated by habitat. This "partitioning" reduces competition for similar food resources. Such is the case with the House Finch, the Purple Finch, and Cassin's Finch—all residents of western North America. The House Finch is most common in the drier, warmer lowlands, while the Purple Finch is found mainly in the moist forests on the lower mountain slopes. Cassin's Finch prefers the high-altitude fir and pine forests.

**Identification**  6–6½". The male shows a characteristic rose-colored crown, breast, and rump; otherwise, it is brown-streaked above with a white belly. The female is brown-streaked above with a heavily streaked white belly. Males may be distinguished from the similar Purple Finch by the sharp demarcation between the rose crown and brown nape.

**Voice**  A rich, high-pitched, fairly lengthy warble. Gives a high, 3-syllable call note.

**Habitat**  Open coniferous woodlands at high elevations.

**Range**  From British Columbia south to westernmost Texas; breeds in the northern part of its range.

174

### House Finch *Carpodacus mexicanus*

Originally a western species, the House Finch was introduced in the 1940s to the East Coast, where it has expanded and established itself across a broad front. In the West, the House Finch has also displayed its adaptable nature by finding a niche in the newly created suburban areas that were once fir forests. The House Finch exploits a wide variety of food items, including seeds and insects.

**Identification**   5–5½". The male is brownish, with the forehead, eyebrow, rump, throat, and breast orange to deep rose-red; it has a grayish-buff belly and flanks heavily streaked with brown. The female is similar but lacks red and is distinctly streaked below, with no conspicuous head pattern.

**Voice**   A burry, canary-like warble, usually ending with an ascending *zeeee*. Call note is a hard *chirp*.

**Habitat**   Cities and residential areas; also chaparral, deserts, and weedy fields.

**Range**   In the West, from British Columbia south through California and Texas.

176

## Lesser Goldfinch *Carduelis psaltria*

The Lesser Goldfinch is a close relative of the American Goldfinch (see page 180). Although the two species share similar characteristics, the range of the Lesser Goldfinch is much more restricted, being confined to western North America. The male's complex, canary-like song is sung from a perch as well as in flight. He is also well known as a mimic, often appropriating phrases and notes from other bird songs to add to his own medley.

**Identification** 3½–4". Males have a distinctive black crown that is more extensive than the American Goldfinch's black cap. Some males have black backs; others have gray-green backs. There are white wing patches and bright yellow underparts. Females are gray-green above and dull yellow below.

**Voice** A lively, sweet song of trills, twitters, and slurred notes, *kur-lee*, with occasional rough, raspy phrases. Call note is a plaintive, down-slurred *tee-yer.*

**Habitat** Brushy areas and woodland edges.

**Range** Breeds from western Oregon south to Texas and east from Nevada to Colorado.

178

## American Goldfinch *Carduelis tristis*

Goldfinches are regular patrons of thistle-seed feeders throughout the year, but their lively song and animated aerial territorial displays make them especially conspicuous in late spring. During the winter, small flocks are often seen in their roller-coaster flight. They pause in the tops of catkin-bearing trees to feed on the seeds.

Identification
: 4½–5½". The breeding male is bright yellow, with the crown, wings, and tail black; the rump and wingbars are white. The female and nonbreeding male are olive-brown above and buff gray below. There is a trace of yellow on the head and face at any season.

Voice
: A jumble of sweet, twittering notes. Flight note is a sweet *per-chick-o-ree;* also a plaintive *chi-ee.*

Habitat
: Thickets, overgrown pastures, marshy areas, weedy grasslands, and suburban parks and yards.

Range
: Breeds from southern British Columbia and northern Alberta to Newfoundland, south to southern California, Utah, Nebraska, Oklahoma, and South Carolina. Winters throughout most of its breeding range south to Mexico.

180

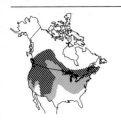

**Evening Grosbeak** *Coccothraustes vespertinus*

The gregarious and boisterous Evening Grosbeak was originally a western species that began colonizing eastern boreal forests around the turn of the 20th century. Great flocks irrupt southward in some years as far as central Texas, where they feed on the buds and seeds of trees, or on sunflower seeds dispensed at suburban birdfeeders.

Identification 7–8½". A stocky bird with a large, greenish-yellow, conical bill. The male has a yellow forehead and eyebrows; its head, upper back, and breast are rich brown. The lower back, rump, and belly are bright yellow; the wings are black with large white patches. The female is grayer.

Voice A disconnected warble. Call note is a loud *cleep* or *cleer;* also a soft clicking note, especially in flight.

Habitat Coniferous and mixed forests; irregularly at suburban birdfeeders in winter.

Range Breeds from British Columbia to Nova Scotia, south throughout the western mountains; also to Minnesota, northern New York, and northern New England. Winters from southern Canada irregularly to the southern U.S.

### House Sparrow  *Passer domesticus*

The House Sparrow was introduced into this country in the mid-1800s for the purpose of controlling noxious insect pests. The species quickly spread and was soon competing with various native species, as well as becoming an agricultural pest. With the decline of agriculture and of the use of horses, a reduction in grain availability caused the numbers of sparrows to decline. Despite this, House Sparrows still occur in practically every town in the United States.

Identification  5¾–6¼". The male is brown above, streaked with black; there is a single bold white wingbar. The head has a gray crown; there is a chestnut nape and a grayish cheek. The throat and breast are black; the rest of the underparts, gray. Females and immature birds are plainer, with brown crowns, a buff stripe behind the eye, and grayish underparts.

Voice  Various twitters and a repeated *chirp, cheep;* also a scolding chatter.

Habitat  Farmland, cities, towns, and suburban areas.

Range  Throughout most of southern Canada and the entire U.S.

184

# Parts of a Bird

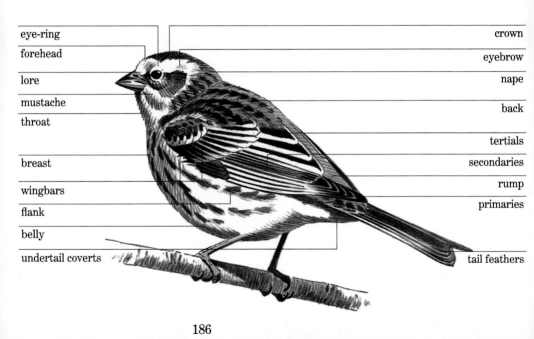

eye-ring
forehead
lore
mustache
throat
breast
wingbars
flank
belly
undertail coverts

crown
eyebrow
nape
back
tertials
secondaries
rump
primaries
tail feathers

# Glossary

**Coverts**
The small feathers covering the bases of usually larger feathers, providing a smooth, aerodynamic surface.

**Crown**
The uppermost surface of the head.

**Eyebrow**
A stripe running horizontally from base of bill above the eye.

**Eye-ring**
A fleshy or feathered ring around the eye.

**Eye-stripe**
A stripe running horizontally from base of bill through the eye.

**Flight feathers**
The long feathers of the wing and tail used for flight. The flight feathers of the wing are composed of primaries, secondaries, and tertials.

**Gorget**
A patch of brilliantly colored feathers on the chin or throat.

**Lore**
The area between the base of the bill and the eye.

**Mandible**
One of the two parts, upper and lower, of a bird's bill.

**Nape**
The back of the head, including the hindneck.

**Primaries**
The longest and outermost (usually 9 or 10) flight feathers.

**Race**
(See Subspecies.)

**Rump**
The lower back, just above the tail.

**Secondaries**
The inner flight feathers that are attached to the "forearm."

**Subspecies**
A geographical population that is slightly different from other populations of the same species.

**Tertials**
The three innermost secondaries closest to the body.

**Wing bar**
A bar of contrasting color on the upper wing coverts.

**Wing stripe**
A lengthwise stripe on the upper surface of the extended wing.

# Index

# Credits

**Photographers**

Ron Austing (63, 99)
Sharon Cummings (159)
Rob Curtis/The Early Birder
(75, 85, 97, 105)

DEMBINSKY PHOTO ASSOCIATES:
Anthony Mercieca (55)
Rod Planck (161)
George E. Stewart (181)

Jeff Foott (Front Cover, 91)
Chuck Gordon (39)
G.C. Kelley (115, 121, 171)
Harold Lindstrom (95, 185)
Bates Littlehales (103)
Charles W. Melton (49)
C. Allan Morgan (43, 53, 59,
71, 79)
Arthur & Elaine Morris/Birds As
Art (31, 93, 123, 133, 139, 157)
James F. Parnell (67)

PHOTO/NATS, INC.:
Sam Fried (177)
Dr. Charles Steinmetz, Jr. (165)

Rod Planck (183)
Jean Pollock (41)
Betty Randall (45, 169)

ROOT RESOURCES:
Anthony Mercieca (147, 149)

Johann Schumacher Design
(73, 113)
Robert C. Simpson (24-25,
129, 167)
Brian E. Small (125)
Hugh P. Smith, Jr. (29, 47, 51, 111,
117, 119, 145, 155)
Tom J. Ulrich (37, 69, 77, 131, 135,
137, 141, 173, 175, 179)
Jim Yuskavitch (89)
Larry West (61, 81, 87, 107)
Paul Zimmerman (3, 27, 35, 65)
Tim Zurowski (33, 57, 83, 101, 109,
127, 143, 151, 153, 163)

Cover Photograph: Cassin's Finch
by Jeff Foott
Title Page: Northern Flicker by
Paul Zimmerman
Spread (24-25): Mourning Doves
by Robert C. Simpson

**Illustrators**

Range maps by Paul Singer
Drawing by Barry Van Dusen
(186)
Silhouette drawings by
Douglas Pratt and Paul Singer

The photographers and
illustrators hold copyrights to
their works.

191

## Staff

This book was created by
Chanticleer Press.
All editorial inquiries should
be addressed to:
Chanticleer Press
568 Broadway, Suite #1005A
New York, NY 10012
(212) 941-1522

**Chanticleer Press Staff**
Founding Publisher:
Paul Steiner
Publisher: Andrew Stewart
Managing Editor: Edie Locke
Production Manager:
Deirdre Duggan Ventry
Assistant to the Publisher:
Kelly Beekman
Text Editor: Carol M. Healy
Consultant: John Farrand, Jr.
Photo Editor: Lori J. Hogan
Designer: Sheila Ross
Research Assistant:
Debora Diggins

Original series design by
Massimo Vignelli.

To purchase this book, or other
National Audubon Society
illustrated nature books,
please contact:
Alfred A. Knopf, Inc.
201 East 50th Street
New York, NY 10022
(800) 733-3000